Decoding
the Mystery
of Life

1:1
answersingenesis
Petersburg, Kentucky, USA

ISBN: 1-60092-257-0

For more information, write:
Answers in Genesis
PO Box 510
Hebron, KY 41048

Written by: Stacia McKeever
Edited by: Becky Stelzer
Illustrations by: Dan Lietha
Layout by: Diane King

Printed in China

www.AnswersInGenesis.org

Decoding the Mystery of Life

Many people have questions about life.

Who am I?

Where did I come from?

What happens when I die?

Am I just another animal?

But there's no mystery when we know where to look for the answers!

The Bible has the answers!

God is the creator of everything. He created the heavens and the earth in six actual days just 6,000 years ago. And He has given us a book that tells us about Himself and His creation. That book is the Bible. It tells us the truth about the past so that we can know where we came from and where we're going.

When we read God's words in the pages of the Bible, we can decode the mystery of life and find the answers we seek!

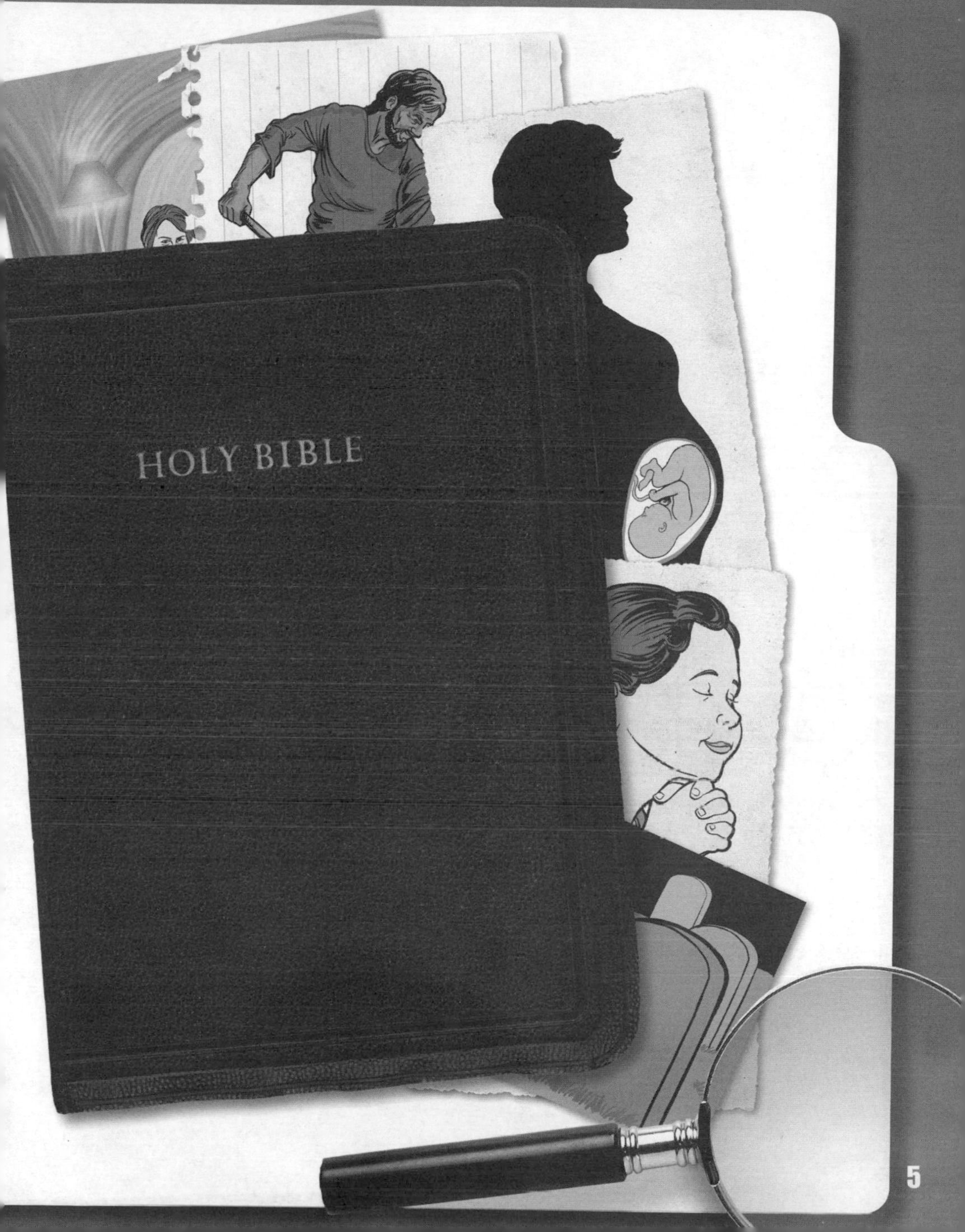
HOLY BIBLE

Where did we come from?

Some people say that we evolved over millions of years from a tiny organism. But there's no mystery when we read the Bible!

In the beginning, God created a beautiful universe that He called "very good" (Genesis 1:31). In six days, by His spoken word, He created light, space, time, water (Day 1), sky (Day 2), dirt, plants, trees (Day 3), sun, moon, stars (Day 4), and swimming creatures and flying creatures after their kind (Day 5).

On the sixth day, God created animals after their kind and the very first people, Adam and Eve. They didn't come from a tiny organism or evolve from an ape-like ancestor. God created them in His very image (Genesis 1:26).

Am I just another animal?

Some people say that we're just another animal, like the monkeys or the apes. But there's no mystery when we read the Bible!

God created people and animals on the same day (Genesis 1:24–31). But He created them differently. God created Adam from the dust of the ground, and then He created a helper for Adam from his side. God created Adam and Eve in His own image.

He gave them several jobs to do. They were to take care of the garden and also to rule kindly over the animals. God also gave them a command to follow and said there would be consequences for disobedience.

The Apostle Paul said that humans are different from animals: All flesh is not the same flesh, but there is one kind of flesh of men, another flesh of animals, another of fish, and another of birds (1 Corinthians 15:39).

We're not just another animal (although we have many features in common with them). We were created in God's very image and have special jobs to do that please our Creator.

Do I share an ancestor with apes?

Some people claim that people and apes share a common ancestor. But there's no mystery when we read the Bible!

God created land animals (such as the apes and monkeys) after their kind on Day Six. Just a little while later, on the same day, God created humans. This happened as soon as God spoke the words about 6,000 years ago, not over millions of years. Ape-like creatures didn't slowly turn into humans over long periods of time—God created apes after their kind, and He created people after their kind.

It's true that we share some similarities with apes (for example, apes and humans both have thumbs that help them grasp objects).

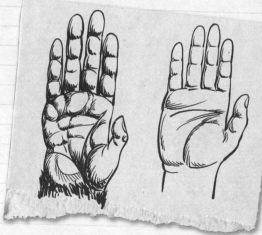

But, there are also many differences.

Humans and apes walk differently.

Their feet are different.

Their jaws and faces are different.

But most importantly, humans were created in the image of their Creator; apes weren't. And Jesus came to earth to save humans, not apes.

Were there really ape-men?

Some people claim that ape-men were links between an ape-like ancestor and humans. But there's no mystery when we read the Bible!

Since we know that God created apes and humans separately on the same day, we can know there aren't any "missing links." These "ape-men" are either fully apes, fully human, or mixed up bones from both apes and humans.

✓ Lucy (*Australopithecus afarensis*)—"Lucy" is one of the more famous "missing links." But these bones were actually from some type of chimpanzee that lived in trees.

✓ Neanderthal man—This group of "ape-men" were actually humans—our relatives! Some lived in caves, and they knew how to make stone tools and worked with leather. They made musical instruments and knew how to fix broken bones.

✓ Piltdown man—This "ape-man" was actually just a hoax, a mixture of human and ape bones. The skull was human, while the jawbone was from an ape.

When we see pictures of ape-men, we can take the time to examine the facts more closely. And we can always know that God created apes, and God created humans, but God didn't create ape-men!

Who were the cave people?

Some people say that our ancestors were ape-like creatures who lived in caves. But there's no mystery when we read the Bible!

Cave people were simply people who lived in caves. The Bible tells us that Lot and his daughters lived in a cave (Genesis 19:30). The Israelites also sometimes hid in caves (Judges 6:2; 1 Samuel 13:6).

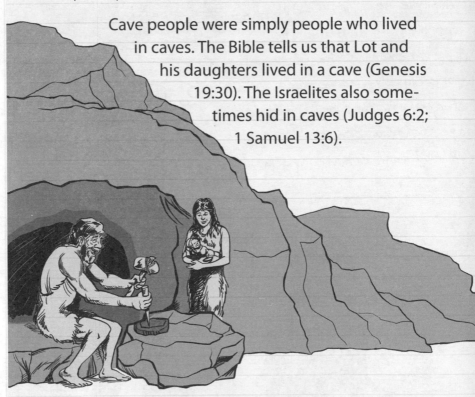

In fact, some people today still live in caves or in houses cut into the side of a hill. In the town of Coober Pedy in South Australia, where opals are mined, it's so hot that some miners live in underground houses. Real live "cavemen" with TV sets!

How smart were our ancestors?

Some people say that our ancestors weren't very smart. But there's no mystery when we read the Bible!

From the Bible we learn that the first people were intelligent from the very beginning. Adam gave names to the animals, so he knew how to speak and be creative (Genesis 2:15–24). It also seems that he knew how to write (Genesis 5:1). He was able to talk with God right from the beginning (Genesis 1:26–30). Adam definitely didn't develop slowly from an unintelligent ape-like ancestor!

Adam's children and grandchildren also had many abilities. They cared for animals, farmed the land, built cities, created and played musical instruments, and worked with metal (Genesis 4:3–4, 17–22). About 1,600 years later, Noah was capable of building a boat that survived a worldwide Flood. And his children and grandchildren became the founders of many nations (Genesis 10–11). They built pyramids, kept meticulous calendars, and built amazing navigational devices.

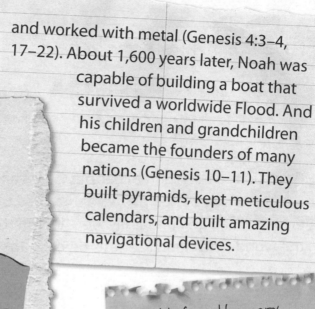

Right from the very beginning, humans have been intelligent, reflecting the intelligence of their Creator!

Are all humans related?

Some people say that there are different races of people. But there's no mystery when we read the Bible!

God created the first two people, Adam and Eve, about 6,000 years ago. Their descendants filled the earth. Later, only Noah and his family were left on the earth after the worldwide Flood (Genesis 6–9). Noah's children and

grandchildren were scattered over the face of the earth after God confused their languages at Babel (Genesis 10–11). From these people came all the tribes and nations that exist today.

The Bible says that the Lord "has made from one blood every nation of men to dwell on all the face of the earth, and has determined their preappointed times and the boundaries of their dwellings" (Acts 17:26).

We're all related! Whether we have dark skin or light skin, curly hair or straight hair, we're all part of Adam and Eve's family. And those who receive the gift of eternal life are part of God's family forever!

Is human life precious?

Some people say that it's okay to take the life of another human being because human life isn't precious. But there's no mystery when we read the Bible!

We're all human, from the time we're conceived until the day we die (see, for example, Jeremiah 1:5; Ecclesiastes 11:5; Luke 1:41). Each life is a precious gift from God (Psalm 127:3–5) and bears His image. And God says not to murder another human being (Exodus 20:13). We have no right to destroy an innocent life, whether old or young.

Only the Creator (and those to whom He delegates it) has the authority to give and take life.

Instead, we need to protect every life—from
the tiniest baby in his mommy's tummy to the oldest
person alive today. We also need to protect and
care for those who are sick, disabled, or suffering.
We are to love our neighbor as we love ourselves
(Mark 12:30-31).

Am I really fearfully and wonderfully made?

Some people claim that we're just the result of accidents that have happened over millions of years. But there's no mystery when we read the Bible!

God says that we're fearfully and wonderfully made (Psalm 139:13–16). He has carefully designed every part of our body to work together marvelously.

✓ Tears—Every blink carries tears from the gland that rests against our eyeball. Tears help keep our eyes moist, wash away dust, and kill bacteria that try to live on our eyeball.

✓ Appendix—Our appendix is very useful. It helps to keep us healthy! It controls the bacteria that live in our intestines and help digest our food. And it also makes antibodies, which help fight off bad bacteria that get into our bloodstream.

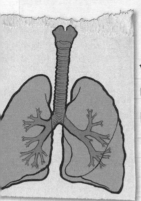

✓ Lungs—Lungs have a layer of tiny hairs that move mucous upward toward the throat, trapping dust and toxins and keeping our lungs healthy.

✓ Hair—We have an estimated 100,000 hairs just on our head. And the Lord knows the exact number (Matthew 10:30)! All hairs are covered with a layer of flattened dead cells (called the cuticle) that help to keep the hair from knotting up. Under the microscope the cuticle looks like overlapping shingles or roof tiles.

✓ Feet—Our feet are made of 52 bones and 250,000 sweat glands that excrete as much as a half-pint of moisture every day. Feet enable us to walk, balance, and hold our skeleton up. Our feet adjust their shape and structure depending on what we're doing. The Bible says that the feet of those who bring the good news of the gospel are beautiful (Romans 10:15)!

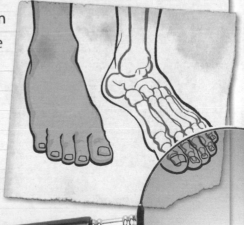

Am I special?

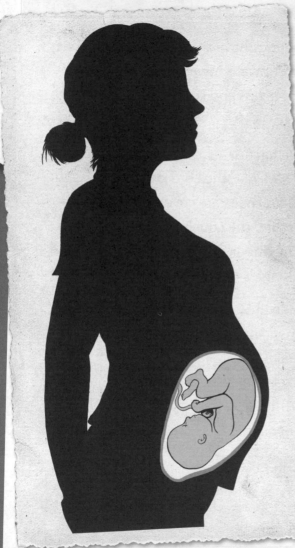

Some people say that we're nothing special—just a collection of molecules. But there's no mystery when we read the Bible!

God created you in His image (Genesis 1:26–28). He carefully formed and shaped you in your mommy's tummy (Psalm 139:13–16). You are a blessing from the Lord (Psalm 127:3–5). He cares about meeting your needs (Matthew 6:25–34).

He wants you to care for His creation (Genesis 1:26–28), have fellowship with Him, and bring Him glory in everything you do (1 Corinthians 10:31). He wants you to love Him and obey His commands (John 14:15–31).

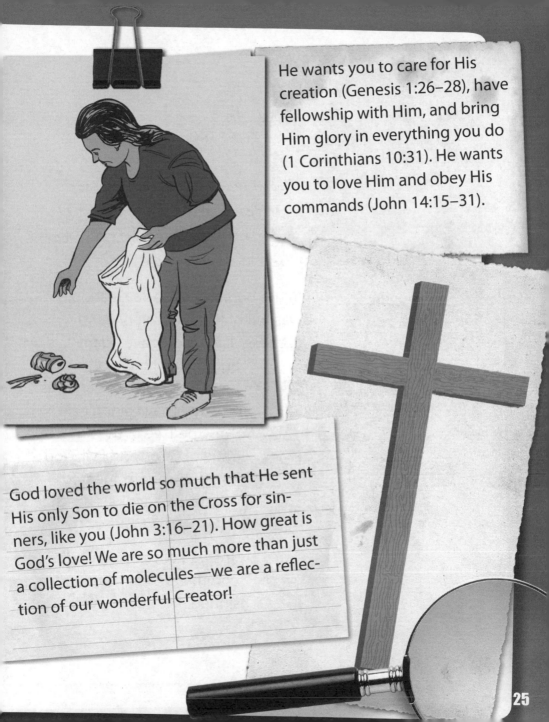

God loved the world so much that He sent His only Son to die on the Cross for sinners, like you (John 3:16–21). How great is God's love! We are so much more than just a collection of molecules—we are a reflection of our wonderful Creator!

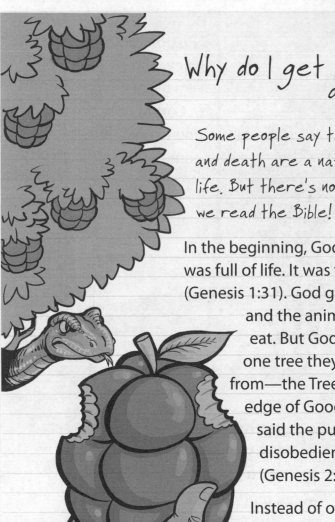

Why do I get sick and die?

Some people say that sickness and death are a natural part of life. But there's no mystery when we read the Bible!

In the beginning, God's creation was full of life. It was very good (Genesis 1:31). God gave Adam, Eve, and the animals plants to eat. But God said there was one tree they couldn't eat from—the Tree of the Knowledge of Good and Evil. God said the punishment for disobedience was death (Genesis 2:17).

Instead of obeying God's command, Adam and Eve sinned. They disobeyed

God's command and ate from the forbidden tree. Because of their sin, God placed a curse on His creation and sentenced them to death (Genesis 3). Since that time, each person is born a sinner and disobeys God (Romans 3:23).

Sickness, suffering, and sorrow are all part of the curse of death that came as the result of sin. It's very sad to see what our sin has done. But there's Good News!

How can I have eternal life?

Some people claim that there is no life after death. But there's no mystery when we read the Bible!

Each of us has disobeyed God (Romans 3:23). We all deserve to be eternally separated from God in a terrible place called hell (Romans 6:23). But God offers us a wonderful gift—life with Him in heaven forever!

God sent His son, Jesus Christ, to earth. Jesus lived a perfect life. But He was put to death on the Cross, paying the

penalty for sin on behalf of mankind. He rose again three days later, showing that God had accepted His sacrifice. When we repent of our sins and believe that Jesus died in our place, we can receive the gift of salvation from our sin (Acts 20:21; Ephesians 2:8–9; Romans 10:9–10).

We become a child of God forever!

What is my purpose?

Some people say that there is no purpose in life. But there's no mystery when we read the Bible!

God has called each of His children to do good works (Ephesians 2:1–10). These good works don't earn us salvation, but are the result of our salvation. We should want to please God and obey His commands because we love Him (John 14).

As part of God's family, we each have a special job to do—some teach, some encourage, some sing, some help others. He has given each of His children important gifts that we are to use for His glory (Matthew 4:14–16). In order to know what He wants us to do, we need to read and study His Word (2 Timothy 3:16–17).

Mystery solved!

When we have questions about life, we need to remember that we have the book from the Giver of Life. The Bible is God's written revelation to us, and we can trust it to tell us the truth about life because God never lies. There's no mystery when we read the Word of God!